Attention Without Deficit

Jenice Moffett

BookLeaf
Publishing

India | USA | UK

Made with ❤ on the BookLeaf Publishing Platform
www.bookleafpub.in
www.bookleafpub.com

Dedication

To every woman battling the immense experiences of ADHD: Your journey is your own, but I hope this collection empowers you to accept your authentic self with pride, humor, and resilience.

Preface

During the height of the pandemic, I experienced not only a shift in the world around me, but also a crashing of my internal capacity. I was promoted. I had just purchased a home. I was working and being a full time mom from the confines of my new home. I was single and thriving, then out of nowhere... I hit a brick wall. Although there were comforts in being in my own space, I quickly realized life required a hell of a lot more out of me, and the systems I built for myself years before no longer served me in this new stage in life. I began seeing a therapist as well as a psychiatrist to finally express the feelings I had struggled with for years and to receive a diagnosis in hopes to understand myself more.

This experience alone set me on a journey of self reflection, acknowledgement, ownership, and transformation. The reality was that everything I wanted to be as a woman was affected by ADHD. It wasn't JUST my forgetfulness- locking keys in cars, forgetting assignments, leaving cabinets open. It was also my avoidance of chores, mismanaged relationships, severe PMS symptoms, and spiraling (courtesy of anxiety). How could I be the powerful leader at work that everyone could rely on? How could I be a responsible parent and role model for my daughter? How could I be the thoughtful friend who answered phone calls and planned outings? How could I certainly be anyone's wife?! The more I unpacked the issues that plagued me, I found my strengths, better systems, healthy relationships, and confidence when living authentically.

This collection expresses the rollercoaster of my experiences- pre-diagnosis, at diagnosis (at 35 years old), and post diagnosis. The attention given to this collection is without deficit. I refuse to view the beauty of the words on each page to being deficient in any way.

To my readers who have never struggled with ADHD but have felt "deficient" at times, I hope this collection inspires you to embrace the struggle in order to find the power of your truth. Neurodivergence or any other diagnosis does not define you. It will shape you, but you are the author of your own narrative. Or poem.

With full attention,
Jenice

Acknowledgements

To my husband who took the time to learn and grow alongside me, I thank you for the high regard in which you hold me and for being vocal about what I have to offer the world. I am fortunate to call you my body double for life.

1. I Do

Bells will be ringing, glad glad-
wait that's Christmas!
Oops, my bad

But baby, you're my gift today
Wedding bells are the ones that play
I thought of EVERYTHING to make you smile
Even down to the timestamps of the song as we make it
down the aisle
Then here it comes like a wrecking ball
The spiraling moments, starting with "girl, don't fall!"
I tried on enough dresses to make your head spin
But now I'm acting like it wasn't giving goddess FTW!

"Do I walk in now? Did I step into the door too late?
Will they notice that coming in on that word was a
mistake?"
My veil sits just as planned
And I glance up at my fine ass man
I see him beaming with joy
And a few remarks that make me a little less coy

His hands lightly move up towards his chest
As he motions for me to slow up- what a mess

"How did I forget to take the step 1, 2 step 1, 2 pace?!
Please don't let me show the panic on my face!"

Somehow, some way, I burst into laughter
Because when I looked into his eyes, nothing else
mattered
I'll admit my mind felt a slight rattled
As the officiant seemed to enjoy his own ramble

Then the time came when we expressed our vows
And I must admit they were so good we should have
taken bows
The universe was unmatched when it sent me my boo
And I thank God for getting me from "girl don't fall" to
"yes, I do!"

2. F is for

Ruminating on the state of your mind
In hopes the search results in a glorious find
The potential joy of dotting all Is and crossing all Ts
Would be a scintillating victory for everyone else you
must please
...To be free from Forgetting...

"Scratch that out, cover this up."
No one will know if you quickly disguise the hiccup.
Find that system to ensure it never happens again
And require people to acknowledge your every win
...To be free from Failure...

Shame sharpens its knife against the coldest stone
Its shine glares as it aims to slice through bone
It never grazes your skin but lingers in sight
As a reminder to keep certain pieces of you hidden from
light
...To be free from Fear...

At sunrise, you gather yourself and flaunt your stuff
Like a chickadee's chest in an upright puff
From mini accolades to boastful awards
Keep foraging it all; not depending on what memory

records

...To be free enough to say F It...

"It's a buzzword. It's an excuse (to name what you won't do)."

"You're being lazy. You're inconsistent (blaming anything but you)."

What you say to society is "I'm your wildest dream!

I'm the creative problem solver everyone needs on their team."

...To be free enough to say F You...

3. GNO Recipe

Step 1.

Keep it last minute to avoid overthinking.

Step 2.

Purchase liquid courage for the pregame drinking.

Step 3.

Allow inhibitions to fall second by second with each sip.

Step 4.

Blast the music as you slide into a banger that makes heads whip.

Step 5.

Be that girl! Crack the jokes! Smile! Dance!

Step 6.

Let that aura free, making them wish they had a chance.

Step 7.

Stand on girl code- gas them up, keep them safe, ask what move's next.

Step 8.

Send the "made it home" message just to see that's the last time you text.

4. I Keep Masking

Smile and nod with affirmation
That I heard every word in that last conversation
Scrambling to make notes as swift as the words flow
Knowing that in minutes many pieces are sure to go
Alarms set to break the hyper focus or daydream
All to show up for those who don't hear my brain scream

No one notices, it's like magic
Every day filled with hocus pocus- I keep masking

"Wow! You're so structured!" colleagues will gloat
"You're the poster child for patience- through problems
you float!"
I smile with pleasure because the way my chest tightens
doesn't show
I could be on the verge of a heart attack and the world
would never know

No one notices, it's like magic
Every day filled with hocus pocus- I keep masking

Meetings with voices competing for shine
Run like nails across a chalkboard at the top of my mind
Inner anxiety and spiraling doesn't pause for the 9-5

So I take deep breaths and tell myself I'll survive

No one notices, it's like magic
Every day filled with hocus pocus- I keep masking

Until

I'm home and it all unfolds
The mask crumbles as I come to a crossroads
I'm home where I'm supposed to be free
But when I cross the threshold, more people need me
I make mistakes and frustrations are more apparent
But at least my feelings of self perception aren't
transparent

No one notices the abhorrence of self, it's like magic
Every day affirmations to rebuild- I keep masking

5. BAWSE

Like a BAWSE, I am...

Bold,
And I dare anyone to tell me I'm not cold

Assertive,
And easily tire from being supportive

Willing,
But sometimes by way of pilling

Solutions-oriented
Because all of the problems are augmented

Executive
Without dysfunction; it's just nonconsecutive

6. Chef's Kiss

Compliments to the chef for cooking something special up!
It's like He took his time, and never once had a hiccup.
The ingredients... were they locally sourced?
Or were they smuggled from distant lands- coursed?

Al bacio! Thank you to the hands that manipulated and molded.
Al bacio! Thank you to the Spirit who guided the blindfolded.
A sprinkle of this, a dash of that;
A cup of wonder for the perfect format!

Share the ingredients? One could never.
My chef is discrete, now and forever.
I evolve, but let's say my roux is the same;
New herbs and spices- no change to the flame.

He gave careful consideration of how one flavor affects another,
So I know the salty and bitter notes dance to compliment each other.
I do not question it- It'd be a blunder if I attempted this myself.

Limited vision- who knows why He pulled that secret sauce off the shelf?

I'm not me without it;
Blasphemy to doubt it.
Divergent for sure;
Chef's kiss mi amor!

7. Big Pimping

Oh the trouble I've caused
'Cause I never need them.
Love sounds good
But what's the true reason?

If I ask, my heart's cold-
I've got no passion.
Thinking I'm Cruella
Or a cold assassin.
Yes I leave them-
Quite quick, to be frank.
No remorse or worry;
Just deposits in the bank.

Not because I'm **big pimping**-
I hate waiting
And have no patience
For their future aching
About where I am
And why I don't hold hands;
Or my outer thoughts vocalizing
How I wish it were a one night stand.

If I wasn't honest, baby

I'd be in your Mercedes
Spending all your money daily
But I'd rather be a lady.

I'm not **big pimping**-
Just a girl who'd rather live alone
Than be overstimulated
 By their desire to cling on.

8. Kitchen Witch

Deep focus and intent coupled with intuitive freedom;
The kitchen is my altar, offering anything from suya to
edam.
Enchanting fragrances of complexity dance on my palate
As nature's bounty renders intoxication from a mere
shallot.
No true spells, but the creations have the power to heal
As intuition leads with love in potent doses of a meal.

I swirl, I float, I flick, I stir- concoctions I beautifully
craft.
No witch am I; just creating magic on my very first draft.
It's this gift I have- to engage in the ritual of cooking
With great purpose- especially when no one's looking.
No witch am I; just mixing masterpieces that stir
Those I love with euphoria in hopes it does recur.

9. Spirals

Ever thought about a spiral's direction?
Is its path nuanced like inflections?
Up or down? Back or forth?

All I know is it winds
Then splits-1 becoming 2 minds.
Up or down? Back or forth?

The battle continues until reality slaps
"You're overreacting!" Ok... perhaps.

10. Company

Sit with me! Chat!
Be silent for a while.
Yes, just like that.

I need your company
For the boring moments.
You can call it gluttony.

Don't go away just yet
Even though I snapped
Because your touch was wet.

I need your company
Even in frazzled times;
I just need you, clumsily.

11. Remember

"Remember when we were young
All those mud pies we flung?"
Wish I could instantly scream, "yes!"
But by memory is in distress.

"Remember what you yelled
Last night while tears swelled?"
It seems too convenient but
I'm trying to recall with eyes shut.

"Remember to take these daily,"
And I reply "I got it!" Oh so gayly
Only to fail miserably weeks later
All because this ailment's my anchor.

Please remember later,
Whether busy or quiet.
Please remember later
So no one goes silent.
Please remember later
To avoid their contempt.
Please remember later
Because the ailment's nonexempt.

12. Super

They say special, I say super.
Who's better than me?
Who can generate ideas
At lightning speed?

The say special, I say super.
Who's more visionary, dear?
I inspire love and change
Without invoking fear.

They say special, I say super.
Who can walk among them all?
From queens to commoners
My stance never falls.

They say special, I say super.
Who can create like me?
Before a sentence is finished,
I transform them from plains, to mountains, to sea.

Superpowers-
I have them.
Special doesn't do enough.

So when you speak of me,
Tell them I'm all super, no bluff.

13. Sweet Mornings

I long for the mornings where no alarms wake me-
The luxury of wondering what I should do
Or determining if I should just be.

Ethereal awakenings, I am able to savor
Instead of rushing to beat the clock.
The stillness and calm makes me feel safer.

Sweet mornings I do crave to revel in-
The syrup of dawn dripping upon my lips
With sprinkles of birds chirping tickling my skin.

Not often am I able to delight in this treat,
But, sweet mornings, I bask in you each time we meet.

14. Taxing

The cost of it all is taxing;
Every dollar is adding up.
The trials I forgot to cancel
Are driving my costs up.

That dress I eyed last week...
Apparently I purchased it then.
I won't remember to return this one;
Might as well just toss it to a friend.

Where did it all go?
I didn't write out that expense.
I wish I didn't purchase items
I'll just throw away- the nonsense!

You thought the tax was emotional?
I appreciate that recognition,
But this tax is beyond belief!
As I scour my budget; poor addition.

15. Spooky Season

Spooky season is any time of the year
ADHD horrors wreaking havoc I fear
Losing keys right before leaving the house
Locking yourself out and having to call the spouse

Spooky season is always approaching
Along with the feeling of panic encroaching
Buying tickets for the right day but wrong year
Faces from the crowd emerge just to jeer
Getting to your appointment on time but wrong day
Nightmares unraveling as you dream how life may fray

16. Woman to Girl

Let me tell you, woman to girl,
How you may go undiagnosed
But learn to cope so well, others will boast.
You may struggle with anxiety
Or feel bouts of depression creep in.
Don't allow those thieves to tell you you can't win.

Let me tell you, woman to girl,
Your struggles may be overlooked.
Your cover will be stale but complex is your book.
You will want to be perfect, girl.
You'll spend excessive time on tasks.
Give yourself grace and peel away at the masks.

Woman to girl, I'll tell you what they won't-
Being who we are is the conundrum;
This experience can be quite the humdrum.
Fluctuating hormones, your moods will often shift
From puberty to postpartum and even menopause,
Don't wonder why- neurodivergence is the cause.

It's immense some days, I'll tell you no lie;
But from woman to girl, for long, don't you cry.

Knowledge is all you need to ensure you can fly.

17. Mind Over Matter

They say our minds are strong enough
To influence outside factors.
I say my mind is strong enough
To place mind over matters.

All around me people shout
"You got this! Do more!"
Then my mind shuts them out,
Sifting through tasks from the day before.

Mind over matter- why yes,
I agree with the literal, not the notion
Just the build of questions is enough mess
To paralyze me from all motion.

"Did my frown end my relationship?"
"That email- I forgot to press send!"
It takes a while to snap out and catch a grip
Just to realize I missed my turn on West End.

Matters appear one item at time,
But this mind holds it all.
Stress levels ring chime by chime.
Every issue bounces within one big ball.

My psyche psyches me out
Before I can even get started.
Motivation needs time to sprout
Before mind and matter become dearly departed.

18. Dope

Don't crash on me- I'll crash out.
You're my dope- I mean- hope.
Everything right about me
Depends on you

To stay attentive
To organize
To not be so impulsive
To just finish
One assignment
Or my last sentence.

Don't crash on me- I'll crash out.
You're my dope- I mean- hope.
If you don't stay, I'll just chase you
Through all the activities I use to cope.

19. Mom

My mom always fussed
About all the things I forgot
About the chores untouched
She showered me with love
But dealt with my feelings with disgust

She did the best she could
With a girl so misunderstood
The validity of her concerns
Turned into lessons learned

So now I watch my daughter
Who doesn't present as I did
But whose words as clear as water
Sound as familiar as my mother's
Making me feel a second round of slaughter

Don't forget to pick me up
Did you sign my permission slip
My heart is hearing don't F this up
With every reminder she gives.

Who do I remind
Who do I push

What comfort do I find
In being the mom who could

20. Wife

They say when a man finds a wife
He finds him a good thing
But find you one with ADHD
And hit the jackpot: cha-ching!

Her struggles make her nurturing
She's supportive and loving
She knows how to adapt
She'll take her time- no rushing

She gives you all the care
She wishes she received
In times when she needed comfort
Or just a moment of reprieve

Enjoy her time and attention
She'll hyper-focus on you
She'll give you the world
Sit back, enjoy the view.

21. Attention Without Deficit

What's wrong with me? Hmmph.
What's wrong with the world?
We force everyone to be the same
Then put labels on boys and girls.

We grow up as men and women
Who want to be free from molds
But are bound by the same ideals,
Repeating everything we were told.

There's no deficit in this attention
Just a world scared of difference;
A world consumed with hustle
Guided by self interests.

Time was made to be enjoyed;
Brains made to wander,
Spirits designed to explore
To gaze upon, to ponder.

Your systems are with deficit.
Remove the shame from diagnosis.
Be honest about how productivity

And greed have us under hypnosis.

Attention without deficit.
Oppression is the prerequisite.
The world won't share its truth
So, instead, we must sleuth.